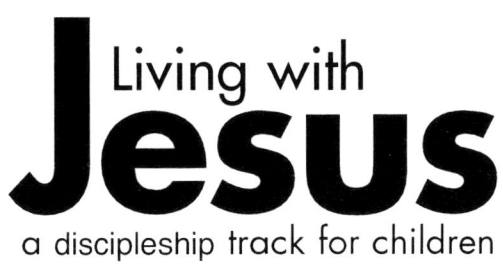

Living with
Jesus
a discipleship track for children

Having faith
Introducing children to a life of faith

Daphne Kirk

Generation 2 generation

First published in 1999 by
KEVIN MAYHEW LTD
Buxhall, Stowmarket, Suffolk IP14 3DJ

Designed by Angela Palfrey
Edited by Helen Elliot

2nd printing in 2004 by
Daphne Kirk
Edited by Lana Robison

0 1 2 3 4 5 6 7 8 9

ISBN 1 84003 340 1
Catalogue No 1500260

Printed and bound in the United States of America

Contact Daphne Kirk by email via her website:
www.gnation2gnation.com

Introduction

Living with Jesus is a tool for discipleship. It can be used in a variety of settings, but perhaps the most effective will be in the context of child and parent.

The adult is named a 'special friend' in the material so this can be applied to a parent or responsible adult.

The following guidelines will help you to achieve the best from the time spent with your child. Meet with one child at a time; each child is different!

1. Anticipate that you will change and grow with the child; apply the material to yourself also.

2. Try to have one session a week with your child (values cannot be changed every day!).

3. *Living With Jesus* aims to stimulate sharing and deepen relationships, so take your time together in a relaxed, quiet environment.

4. The material is not designed to answer questions, but to reveal issues that need to be talked through.

5. If you are not the parent, always gain the permission of the parent. Show them the material. Ask if they would like to join you as you meet with the child. Stay in a place where you can be seen and heard by others, i.e. not behind closed doors.

6. Remember that honest answers are 'right' answers.

7. If you are unsure how to react, or unsure of an answer, it is all right to tell the child that you will talk about it again the next time you meet, and take some time to pray or ask for help.

8. Find creative ways to learn the memory verse, i.e. put actions to it, draw a picture of it, fill in words, make them into plaques, etc.

Remember that this is one of the most important times with your child. You have all the wisdom and anointing of the Holy Spirit available to you. Enjoy your time…have fun and expect Jesus to be at the centre!

To Megan and Harry
and the next generation

My name is: _____

My friend is: _____

My church is: _____

_____

_____

We will meet on: _____

_____

My address is: _____

_____

_____

_____

Contents

1

What is
faith?

What is faith?

Q **What do you think faith is?**

I think **faith** is _____

_____

_____

_____

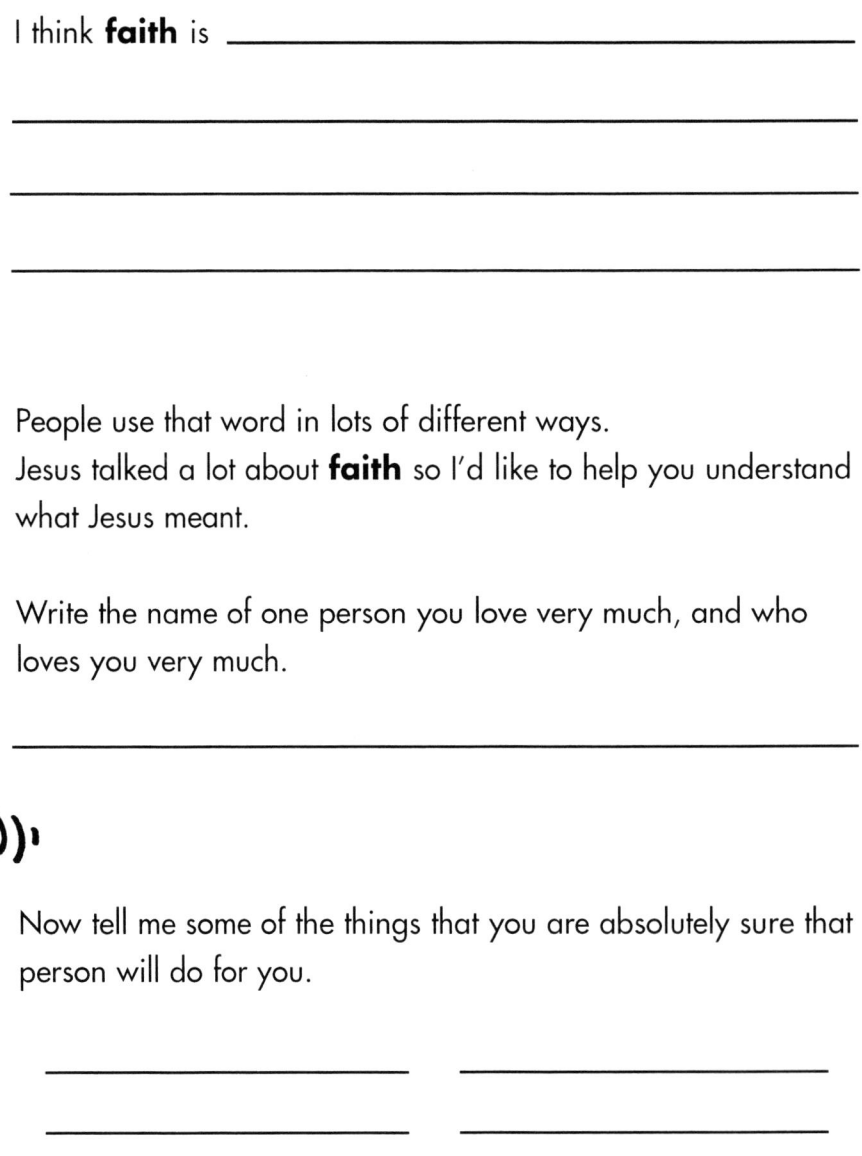

People use that word in lots of different ways.
Jesus talked a lot about **faith** so I'd like to help you understand what Jesus meant.

Write the name of one person you love very much, and who loves you very much.

_____

Now tell me some of the things that you are absolutely sure that person will do for you.

_____   _____

_____   _____

_____   _____

Are you sure they will do those things even if you are not watching them? _____

If you said 'Yes' then you have **faith** that they will do it.

means

'I'll believe it even if I can't see it'

Colour the word 'faith'.

Here are some ways of saying **'faith'** that other children thought of . . .

Knowing it will happen.

I'm sure.

Always saying 'yes' about what the Bible says.

I won't listen if you say lots of reasons why it can't happen.

Q **Can you and your special friend think of some different ways of saying 'faith'?**

Read Hebrews 11:1

Now _ _ _ _ _ _ is being _ _ _ _ _ of what we hope for and _ _ _ _ _ _ _ _ of what we _ _ _ _ _ _ _ _ _ .

Q Sometimes it is easy to believe things.
What things do you believe?

I believe _____

_____

_____

_____

_____

Sometimes we don't believe things.
What things don't you believe?

I don't believe _____

_____

_____

_____

_____

It is good to believe some things and good not to believe other things –

are all the things you believe good things to believe?

_____

Why do you believe them?

_____

_____

I am going to give you a list of statements and I want you to **tick the ones which are good to believe** and **put a cross by the ones which are bad to believe.**

☐ Jesus loves me.

☐ The Bible is only half true.

☐ I am a wonderful person.

☐ Jesus only loves some people.

☐ Jesus is coming back again for me.

☐ My prayers are very important.

If we have faith and believe something even though we can't see it, it is important that our faith is in things that are good and true.

Where can we find out if what we believe is good and true?

In the _ _ _ _ _

14

Memory Verse

● This is your verse to learn this week. You can learn it and then say it to your special friend, or perhaps you could learn it together!

Now faith is being sure
of what we hope for
and certain of what
we do not see.

Hebrews 11:1

More sharing together

1. Ask your special friend to tell you about a time when they really believed (had faith) that something was going to happen and it did.

2. Now you share a time with them when you really believed (had faith) something was going to happen and it did.

3. Each of you think of something different that it is good to believe (have faith for).

Pray together about those two things.

2

Faith without seeing, feeling or touching

Faith without seeing, feeling or touching

Tom and Sue were twins. They asked their friend John to come to their birthday party.

John was very pleased and said that he would give each of them a ball as a present.

Do you think that John would bring the presents as he promised?

_____

Tom thanked John. He was excited because he had lost his ball. He looked forward to the party and made plans to play football with his friends.

Sue was worried. She wondered if John would really buy a ball. She was afraid that he would forget, or that she would not like it. All week she waited anxiously.

Who do you think had faith that they would receive the ball?

_____

Who was sure of something he had not seen?

_____

Tom had **faith**.

Sue was very unsure – she did not have **faith**.

Now let's think about another story.

Read Luke 1:26-31

What did the angel promise Mary? _____

When the angel told Mary that she would have a baby,
could Mary **touch** the baby at that very moment? _____

Could Mary **see** the baby at that very moment? _____

Could Mary **feel** the baby at that very moment? _____

Do you think Mary believed the angel? _____

Do you think she had faith for that baby? _____

Now:

Read Luke 1:38

What did Mary do?

Cross out the wrong answers.

She argued with the angel.

She thought it was a joke.

She cried about it.

She believed the angel.

She had **faith** that it would happen.

Yes . . . Mary believed what God had told her
through the angel, so she had

faith

Mary was **sure** of what the angel had said and
was **certain** about the baby she had not seen.

**What was the name of the
baby that God gave her?** _ _ _ _ _

Look at Luke 1:31

There are things you can have faith for because Jesus has given us promises about them.

Read the end of Joshua 1:5

'I will be _ _ _ _ you, I will _ _ _ _ _ _ _ _ _ _ you.'

Can you see Jesus? _____

Can you touch Jesus? _____

Do you know that He is with you? _____

Will He stay with you all the time? _____

If you said 'Yes' to the last question then you have faith!

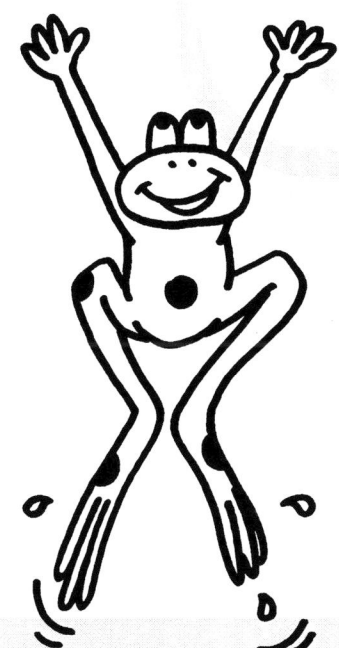

21

Some things that Jesus tells us are hard to believe (or have faith for).
Can you tell me about times when you find it hard to believe
that Jesus is still with you?
You can write about them, or draw a picture

Your special friend will pray with you about these.
But
this is how you can **know** He will love you and stay with
you all the time.

He said He would, and He never, never, never

_____

(put some more 'nevers' along here)

breaks His promises!

Memory Verse

● This is your verse to learn this week. You can learn it and then say it to your special friend, or perhaps you could learn it together!

I am the Lord's servant.
. . . May it be to me
as you have said.

Luke 1:38

1. When we believe Jesus, even if we don't see or feel him, it is called

FAITH

Make your own border round the word 'Faith', colour this in together and make this look very special.

Make a list together of things you can't see, feel or touch but can still believe (have faith) in.

_____

_____

_____

_____

_____

Now thank Jesus together for them.

3

What about other people?

What about other people?

Read Acts 14:8-10

together and draw these pictures . . .

1. A man sat, crippled in both his feet.

2. He was lame from birth and had never walked.

3. He listened to Paul as he was speaking.

4. Paul looked at him and saw he had faith.

What did Paul call out?

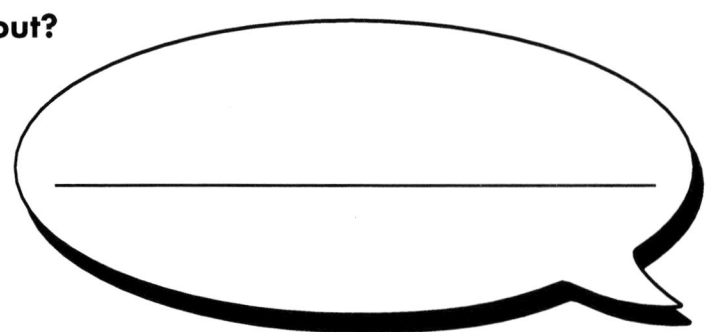

What do you think the crowd who were watching thought?

They thought _____

_____

What did the man do? Draw the picture.

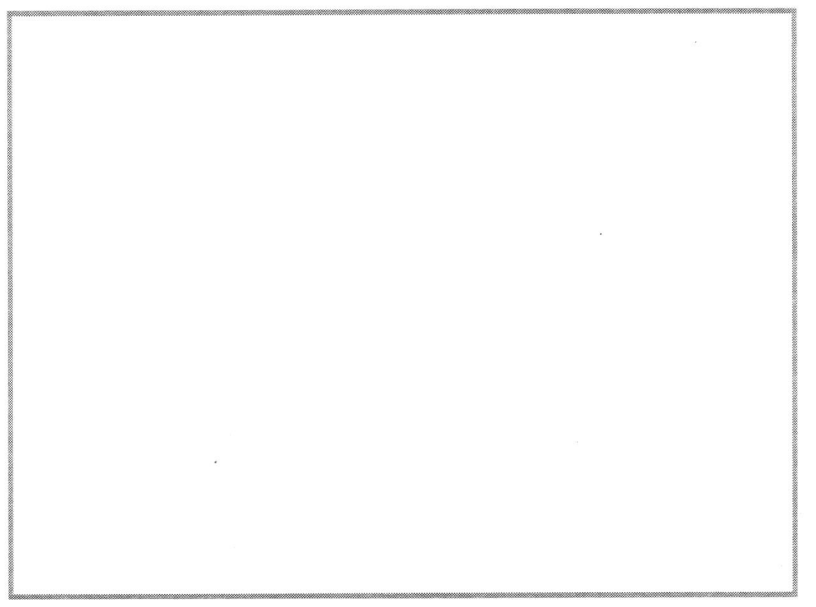

He **jumped**

and he **walked**

Had he ever done that before? _____

Why did he do it this time? _____

_____

27

Paul . . .

spoke Jesus' words

was full of the Holy Spirit

The man . . .

heard Paul

believed (had faith)

obeyed and got up

Sometimes we believe Jesus and other people think that we are stupid.

Should that stop us believing Jesus? _____

Will it be easy to keep believing Him? _____

Are there any people who laugh at you, or call you names because you believe, or have faith in Jesus? _____

Pray with your special friend about this.

If Jesus said it in His Word, the Bible,
then you can keep believing and having
faith even if everyone laughs.
It won't be easy but
with the help of the Holy Spirit you can do it!

Memory Verse

● This is your verse to learn this week. You can learn it and then say it to your special friend, or perhaps you could learn it together!

Faith
without deeds
is dead.

James 2:26

Ask your special friend to tell you about times when they have been laughed at for believing Jesus. What did your special friend do?

Now share together about times when you have both laughed at or thought unkindly about another person.

Both of you say you're sorry to Jesus for those times (if you really mean it).

Pray for each other.

4

Believing that I am special

Believing that I am special

Do you know that . . .

**You are God's
very special child.**

**You are born into
His family.**

You can't see this, but if you are sure of it,

and you are certain it is true – then you are His child by **faith**.

Read Hebrews 13:5b

God has said

'_ _ _ _ _ will I

_ _ _ _ _ you.'

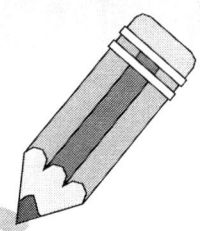

Do you really believe that? _____

Can you see Him? _____

Can you touch Him? _____

How do you know He is there? _____

We know He is there because we have **faith.**

When you are frightened
Jesus is with you.

When you are happy
**Jesus is
with you.**

When you are lonely
**Jesus is
with you.**

I am going to tell you something really special . . .

Children have a lot of faith and adults are told to have faith like children!

Memory Verse

● This is your verse to learn this week. You can learn it and then say it to your special friend, or perhaps you could learn it together!

I will be with you;
I will never leave you.

Joshua 1:5

More sharing together

1. Ask your special friend to tell you about a time when they knew Jesus was with them, though they couldn't see Him.

If that has happened to you, tell your special friend about it.

2. Can you think of someone who is lonely and needs to see Jesus in you, by having a special visit?

3. Arrange to go to see that person together, to show that you love them. Make a card, or a gift, together to take with you.

4. Pray about your visit together.

5

Keeping your faith

Keeping your faith

Now I am going to tell you how to keep your **faith.**

Read your Bible

Listen to people who believe what Jesus says.

Notice the things Jesus does for you.

Remember to thank Him for everything that He has done.

Thank Him for all the things He is going to do for you.

Learn and remember some of the things Jesus has promised.

Let's see how you are both doing with the list that you just read.
Both of you fill in these spaces.

Read your Bible. Do you both read it regularly?

Listen to people who believe what Jesus says.
Who do you both listen to?

Notice the things Jesus does for you.
How many things can you think of that Jesus has done for you
both this last week?

Remember to thank Him for everything that He has done.
How many times have you both thanked Jesus this week?

Thank Him for all the things He is going to do for you.
What can you both think of to thank Him for that you have
not seen yet? (That will be faith!)

Learn and remember some of the things Jesus has promised.
Can you both write down some of Jesus' promises?

Have **faith...**

What does Hebrews 11:1 say?

_____

_____

_____

_____

What do **you** say faith is now that
you have finished reading this book?

_____

_____

_____

_____

Memory Verse

● This is your verse to learn this week. You can learn it and then say it to your special friend, or perhaps you could learn it together!

Because you have seen me
you have believed;
blessed are those who
have not seen and yet
have believed.

John 20:29

More sharing together

1 Talk about your visit to the person who was lonely.

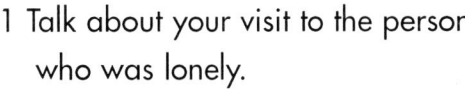

2. Pray for that person again.

3. Pray for each other that Jesus will give you more faith.

4. Now go out together into the street and pray for some of the people in the homes around you. Do this for about ten minutes. As you pray for the different homes, have faith for your prayers to make a difference.

If you have any questions from this book, write them here to ask your special friend.

_____

_____

_____

_____

_____

_____

_____

_____

47